Welcome To Your Nightmares: Your Guide to Finding The Meaning of Monsters, Demons, Snakes, Spiders and Just Plain Scary Dreams

Laura Suzanne

Copyright ©2014 Laura Suzanne

All Worldwide rights reserved. No part of this book may be reproduced or transmitted in whole or in part, in any form whatsoever, without written permission of the author, except by a reviewer who may quote brief passes in a review. Nor may any part of this book be reproduced, stored in a file retrieval system, or transmitted in any form by any means electronic, mechanical, copying, recording or other without written permission of the author.

www.inyourdreamsbooks.com

ISBN: 978-1-944242-20-6

This book is dedicated to Tiger Snell, my faithful companion who was by my side the entire time I was writing this book.

Acknowledgements:

I would like to give thanks to my friends and family for their support throughout this journey. Special thanks to Roy Snell, Victoria Gallagher, Janis Abriel, Leeza Robertson, Stacey Chester, Ellen Greenlee, Juanita Curiel, Helen Baucum, Patrick Curry, Gypsy, Barbara Buchanan, Amy Barilla, Janice Masters, Kim O'Neil, Christine Briscoe, Jennifer Huse, Sara Bruestle, Sharon Savage and, most of all, Mom.

Forward

There is a fantastic place in your mind which you experience each time you fall asleep. A summit within the deepest part of your mind, where extraordinary thoughts happen, where you can give or receive messages through your subconscious mind. Your mind records and remembers every experience you have ever had, including all of your dreams. It stores this information in your subconscious mind. But just how do you make use of that information?

That is exactly what my colleague and friend, Laura Suzanne Snell will help you do as she takes you on an important journey of self-discovery and a deeper understanding of your dreams and what they mean in her new book, "Welcome To Your Nightmares: Your Guide to Finding The Meaning of Monsters, Demons, Snakes, Spiders and Just Plain Scary Dreams".

Every time you fall asleep, you dream. Your dream time is like an untold story, the true story underneath the surface, about what's really happening in your life.

By reading this engaging book, you will soon realize that YOU ARE a dream interpreter and this book will help you decipher the hidden meaning contained within the dreams.

All of your dreams are thoughts from your own unconscious mind, so of course, it stands to reason that they are somehow connected to who you are and your own reality. Some dreams make sense to you right away, you get them, and know why you had them. It's those dreams that do not make sense right away, that leave you puzzled, that have a deeper meaning which you are about to find out in "Welcome To Your Nightmares: Your Guide to Finding The Meaning of Monsters, Demons, Snakes, Spiders and Just Plain Scary Dreams".

Having been in the personal growth industry since the late 90's, I first came to know Laura through the dream interpretation column she wrote for the Las Vegas Weekly. Impressed with her deep intuition and abilities, I felt she would make a tremendous impact as a guest on the radio show I hosted, "Hyptalk."

As it turned out, Laura brought such a special charm, insight and wisdom to the show that I later asked her to be my co-host.

Laura has always had wonderful intuition and skill and so it's no surprise she decided to utilize her special gift and pass along this incredible wisdom to you as a way to help you gain self-awareness and clarity through recalling and interpreting your own dreams.

While, there are other books on the market that provide basic dream meanings, this book not only provides some of the most common dream definitions, but it goes well beyond that.

The truth is, as you'll quickly realize in "Welcome To Your Nightmares: Your Guide to Finding The Meaning of Monsters, Demons, Snakes, Spiders and Just Plain Scary Dreams", your dreams have their own significant, unique and personal meaning to you.

You will gain more than knowledge. You will gain the wisdom of how to decode the secret language of your subconscious mind and your dreams will now take on a whole new dimension and become more of a learning tool for you.

I can tell you as a Certified Clinical Hypnotherapist since 1999, there is much more to you that you are fully aware of. Gaining awareness of who you really are however, is one of the great benefits worth exploring as you delve into this fascinating area of your mind through the insights presented to you in your dreams.

As you read this book, you will come to a place, as I did, which creates a feeling of confidence that you really are capable of interpreting your own dreams.

Laura provides ample examples and tools to help you do just that. With a little time, practice and patience, you'll be looking at the signs revealed to you within your dreams and gaining a deeper understanding about yourself as a result.

As you progress and get better at interpreting your dreams, it will simply become more natural for you to ask yourself the proper questions, instantaneously, such as the questions Laura suggests in "Welcome To Your Nightmares: Your Guide to Finding The Meaning of Monsters, Demons, Snakes, Spiders and Just Plain Scary Dreams"and to be able to quickly draw your own conclusions from your internal resources within and from your life experience to help guide you to know what your dreams are about the moment you do remember them.

With Laura's gift of being empathic, I couldn't be happier that she has decided put all her insights down in this wonderful book to assist you in your journey and I know it will help you grow in love, health, and wealth.

--Victoria Gallagher
http://www.hyptalk.com

Introduction

Dreaming is something that everyone experiences. This book is your guide to understanding your dreams and what they mean. This book was originally a compilation of newspaper columns featuring dreams submitted to me by my readers and my interpretation of their dreams. Being that there were well over 100 dreams in the collection, I chose to make this into three separate books broken down by category. This book, the second in a three-part series, is all about monsters, devils, demons, spiders, snakes and just plain scary dreams. I have used real-life dreams from actual readers to illustrate my points and my interpretations of these dreams. There will also be exercises for you, the reader, to give personal meaning to your dreams and decode the messages from your subconscious mind.

Table of Contents

Chapter One: The Importance of Your Dreams and Why You Have Them

In this chapter we will discuss dreams and why they are important, as well as some steps for making interpretation simple.

Chapter Two: The Anatomy of a Nightmare

In this chapter we will discuss what it means to have a nightmare and night terror from a physiological and psychological perspective, as well as how nightmares can actually be beneficial.

Chapter Three: Dreams of Demons and Devils

In this chapter we will discuss the appearance of demons and devils in dreams and possible meanings, as well as how to determine if this is a manifestation of your subconscious or an attack, and what to do if it is the latter.

Chapter Four: Dreams of Monsters, Goblins, Scary Clowns, Snakes and Spiders

In this chapter we will discuss the significance of these dream characters, and the role movies play in influencing our dreams.

Chapter Five: Menacing or Opposing Figures in Dreams

In this chapter we will discuss the appearance of menacing or opposing dream figures, and how to decipher the hidden messages they may have for you.

Chapter Six: Just Plain Scary Dreams

In this chapter we will discuss common scenarios that cause fear and anxiety in dreams and how to see the hidden gifts, as well as applying the messages to your waking life.

Chapter Seven: Facing Your Fears Through Lucid Dreaming

In this chapter we will discuss how to use your scary and unpleasant dreams to your greater advantage through lucid dreaming and how to banish those fears for good!

Chapter Eight: Dream Journal Exercises

In this chapter we will explore some different exercises for better dream recall.

Conclusion

Author Bio

Chapter One: The Importance of Your Dreams and Why You Have Them

Everyone dreams. We do not always remember what we dream about, however, we all have dreams when we are asleep. Some dreams are in color while some are in black in white. Some will seem obvious or be very vivid, where others are more vague and elusive, almost uneventful. A dream can often be construed as a nonsensical mishmash of images strewn together that resemble pieces of a puzzle that will never be solved. To have a dream can simply be a brain dump; a subconscious regurgitation of the previous day's events as a method of cleaning house. They can play out like a movie, sometimes scary, sometimes comical, sometimes erotic. At times it can be frustrating and confusing trying to make sense of them, however, the more that you make a conscious effort to connect with them, the easier it gets to truly know their meaning.

To have a dream is tantamount to getting a letter from a trusted friend. You would not even consider just throwing it away unopened, would you? I didn't think so! That is what you are doing when you do not pay much attention or just flat out ignore your dream. It is like deleting an email, status unread, within the body of the letter contains a precious gift which is a message from your higher self delivered via your subconscious mind, expressly for you. The fact that you are reading this book suggests that you have a desire to be more in tune with and to learn from your nightly excursions.

The key to understanding your dreams is to first pay attention and look for the obvious. What stands out? Who were the key players; people, animals, etc in the dream? What was your role? What was the setting; outdoors, building, vehicle, etc? What was the time frame: past, present or future? What was the emotional climate, feeling or sensation in the dream? Try to recall anything and everything that you can remember about the dream, no matter how small or insignificant it may seem at the time. If it was there, and you were aware of it….a lipstick stain on a glass, for example, it is a significant part of the dream and not to be overlooked. You may not understand it now, however, by the time you are finished reading this book, you will have far greater insight into your own dreams.

Your dream is always telling you something about yourself and what is going on in your life, sometimes it will be very simple and obvious, and often times it will appear a bit more cryptic. I have seen which friends I can trust and which ones will disappoint me in a dream. I have been given clues about the intentions of others, and had future premonitions about them all while dreaming. I always take the time to listen to what my dream has to say and how I can apply it to my daily life.

Some dreams will have more meaning to you than others and will make more of an impact. Some are very basic but they always have a meaning no matter how trivial they seem at first. If you dream of roses, for example, that could mean that you are about to "blossom" or "come into bloom" in your personal or professional life. Perhaps you will meet your soul mate or get that big promotion? There are so many symbols and each is subject to your own personal interpretation. Yes, you can certainly look at definitions in a dream book and there are several good ones available. I have my own version available online which you are welcome to look at as well. However, instead of relying on someone else to tell you what your dream means..it is always better to go directly to the source and ask the right question: "What does this dream mean to ME?"

It really is a personal journey unique to the dreamer to decode a dream as the meaning can vary greatly from one individual to another. To see a red rose, for example, would generally be seen as a precursor to romance. Roses are beautiful and they smell great! The color of the rose will have a different meaning, too. Is it red (romance) yellow(friendship) or black (death)? Perhaps to see a rose is your higher self telling you to stop and take a minute to "smell the roses", to be more present and enjoy life more . However, if you work tending a rose garden or in a flower shop, there more be a more mundane aspect to your dream.

With all of the many dreams that were submitted to me via email and in person for interpretation from clients, my job was not to provide them with a canned definition but to help them extract the meaning specific to them. A person who works as a gardener would have a very different take on roses than would a beauty pageant contestant to whom roses are presented as a prize. One might view it as their daily grind perhaps where the other may see it as a reward. What is your definition of a rose? Love them or hate them? Favorite color of rose and why? This will help you to personalize it as it pertains to you. I am here to guide you, however, you are always your own best authority on everything, dream interpretation included.

Chapter Two: The Anatomy of a Nightmare (Night Terrors and Bad Dreams)

Have you ever said to someone "I had the worst dream last night" or uttered the phrase "What a nightmare" in reference to something that happened in your waking state? What is your version of a nightmare? The definition of a nightmare according the Miriam-Webster dictionary is *"a terrifying or unpleasant dream in which the dreamer experiences feelings of helplessness, extreme anxiety, sorrow, etc."* In this chapter I will cover what it means to have a nightmare versus a night terror, how your body functions during sleep and how you can best use a bad dream to your advantage.

When we sleep, our brains do not shut down like a computer does when we turn it off for the evening. Sleep is an active time for the mind, while we may be resting in a bed or on a couch, our bodies can still twist, turn and move. We roll over in our sleep, our bladder signals us that we need to use the restroom causing us to wake up, we throw the covers off when we feel too warm and pull them up when we feel cold... the wheels are definitely turning while we are sleeping. Sleep studies have shown that there is more varied brain activity during the sleep state than when one is awake. (If you find this interesting, there are many books and articles that discuss in great detail the various stages of sleep and brain waves.) I am not going to go into too much depth or detail about sleep, as this is a book on dream interpretation, however, I will touch on some of the basics: The deepest stage of sleep is delta, the middle stage is theta and the waking state is alpha. Dreams occur during the REM (rapid eye movement) sleep cycle, and this includes nightmares.

What is the difference between a nightmare and a night terror? The first is that is that the night terror occurs during the non-REM sleep phase. The second is that a nightmare is something that one will typically have memory of upon waking, whereas with night terrors, there would not be an associated memory. A night terror is something that happens during the transitioning sleep stages, and can also be a reaction to eating spicy food or other physiological stimuli. A friend who had recently quit smoking experienced three weeks of night terrors and poor sleep as the nicotine left his system and he was adjusting to the life of a non-smoker. Many people have reported that heavy or spicy meals too close to bedtime have caused them to have night terrors. Another distinction between the nightmare and the night terror is that when one is having a nightmare, they can easily wake up themselves up from it. A night terror is not as easy to wake up from, and the body will often twitch and jerk, legs and arms may flail… so if your partner kicks or elbows you during the night, they may very well be experiencing a night terror, but will probably have no recollection of it upon waking.

Yet another major difference between the two is that people are more likely to sleepwalk during a night terror or talk in their sleep. I recall when I was a teen, I used to babysit a youngster who would sleepwalk into the living room and stand in front of the TV set. When I tried to talk to him he would not respond, he would simply stare at the screen. I would gently guide him back to bed, as he was not cognizant of the fact that I was speaking to him. His physical body was able to perform the motor function of walking and his eyes were open, however, his mind was somewhere else… "the lights were on but no one was home" applies here.

The main difference, in my opinion, between a nightmare and a night terror is that the night terror is merely a physiological response to a stimulus where a nightmare is something that allows for the psyche to purge itself, as thoughts can be processed and emotions can be released. Nightmares contain elements of the unpleasant and the unwanted so, naturally, it is a relief to wake up from one. Rather than just shaking it off and exclaiming "Whew! I am glad that is over!" and wasting the message, it would behoove you to take a moment and learn from your nightmare.

While the message from your nightmare may seem difficult to understand at first, you can easily identify the feeling or emotion you experienced, and more clues will follow. If you dreamed that you were drowning or a tsunami hit and swept you away, that would suggest a feeling of helplessness or being overwhelmed in some area of your life. Now you can ask yourself "How does this apply to my current situation?" Maybe you recently got a promotion or have taken on more responsibility than you can handle and are buckling under the pressure. Your next question would be, of course, "What do I need to do to remedy this"? You may already know what you need to do or there may be a clue from the nightmare. Perhaps there was a wise man, a horse, a scroll or a staff? These symbols represent people, spirit animals, and tools to assist you on your journey. I would look at them as a wise man for counsel, a horse to carry you, a scroll to direct you and a staff to protect you. These are just a few examples of possible meanings for these symbols; I am certain that you will come up with your own definitions as needed.

Deep feelings of grief and sorrow are a common thread in nightmares, and that is why we will have the tendency to shun them. To dream of a loved one that has passed or a partner who betrayed you is to open old wounds, which causes pain, and we are inclined to avoid anything that hurts. It can be anxiety provoking to dream of losing a child or a partner being unfaithful. The silver lining with the first-case scenario is that if it is a loss that has already occurred, this is your opportunity to experience more complete healing via your dream. The silver lining with the second-case scenario is, if it is a precognitive dream that a loss may be coming, this is your higher self giving you a warning or preparing for you for what may come. Sometimes we can stop the train, sometimes we cannot. If there is something you can do to prevent what you do not want to happen, take immediate action. If it is a circumstance beyond your control, which is sometimes the case, you will be more prepared because you saw it coming.

Your nightmares are of benefit to you, as you will see and experience what you may be repressing or failing to acknowledge in your waking state. It may not be presented in the most appealing package, but just like with any dream, a nightmare can be a gift if you apply the message. There may be a health issue you need to address or a financial investment you should steer clear of. Every negative has a positive intent, and that is true for your nightmares. They are your servants, here to assist you along your path.

Chapter Three: Devils and Demons

To see a devil or demon in a dream can be unsettling for most people, myself included. I know that the motion picture industry has made some absolutely terrifying movies, which many of us can still remember to this day. There are some classic films, like "The Exorcist," "The Omen," "Rosemary's Baby," "Amityville Horror" and countless others that send shivers down one's spine just thinking about them. The more modern films featuring demonic possession are not as scary as the original ones, in my opinion, because they rely heavily on special effects and there is not much of a story line.

The reason I say that these dreams are not pleasant, even for a seasoned dream interpreter like me, is that sometimes they feel like dreams, but often times they seem more lifelike. Demons are real. Yes, Hollywood has done a bang-up job of making them more scary than they already are, however, some of these films were based on true stories and this can and does happen in real life. If you are a skeptic (doubtful if you are reading my book) you can go online and look up case studies about exorcisms for demonic possession performed by Catholic priests worldwide, and it will not be light reading. Demons are real, and they are yucky! I do not like to be attacked by them while awake or visited by them in my dreams. (I have a book coming out soon on house clearing and spirits called "Living Harmoniously with the Spirit World." If you want to read more on this subject, stay tuned, and I will message you when it is released, if I have your email address.)

Those of the Catholic or Christian faith believe in a devil better known as Satan, sometimes referred to as

Lucifer or Beezelbub. He is the iconic red devil with the pitchfork who resides in hell, a fiery pit for the eternally damned. I don't personally have a relationship with any such devil, however, I do know that there is a certain demonic presence that these entities carry with them, and I do not want to engage or entertain them on any level. However, to pretend evil does not exist is naïve. It does exist, and it can surely visit you while asleep or awake.

How it appears to you can come in many forms and have many meanings. You can feel as if you are being attacked while sleeping, or you may just be feeling tempted to do something you feel is not in your best interest by the proverbial "devil on your shoulder." Perhaps the devil you see in your dreams is not an evil spirit trying to take possession, but a disowned part of yourself seeking expression?

Some acknowledge that there are angels and devils, while others simply see dark and light energy. Catholic and Wiccan religions may have different takes, however, I believe it is one and the same. Is the evil within any worse than the evil without? We all contain elements of light and dark or good and evil. Is that devil with a pitchfork in your dream any worse than the bad thoughts or ill feelings you have harbored toward your enemy? C'mon, we all go to the dark side in our minds sometimes. We are all human. Even the self-professed enlightened beings are still subject to fits of road rage and, sometimes, the harder we try to be good or spiritual, the harder the darkest parts of our psyche fight to be acknowledged.

None of us are perfect and we all have a dark side. The more you try to repress something, the more it will need to be expressed, and what better way than through your dreams! With that said, if you feel you are experiencing a demon attack, then by all means break out the Bible and holy water, and ward off those evil spirits! However, if you feel you are simply having a dream that features a devil or demon, chances are it is a part of you that you are not quite comfortable with in your waking life. Where do repressed urges and desires go? To the warehouse of your mind of course; the subconscious. All of the things that you keep private, thoughts that you dismiss, feelings that you do not want to admit even if only to yourself… all of this has to go somewhere, and your subconscious mind is always happy to host.

To see a devil or demon in your dream may be telling you to clean up your act in some way, shape or form. Whatever it is that you are running from, your dreams are the one place where you cannot escape yourself. Whatever it is, just admit there is no need to be ashamed of your innermost thoughts and feelings, no matter how dark or impure they may appear. It is time to delve even deeper within your psyche and ask what this dream character, devil or demon is trying to tell you that you are not willing to look at. Do you have an addiction? Are you being dishonest in some way? These are questions for you to ask of yourself privately. They do not have to be shared nor do you need to sit in judgment of yourself if they feel unpleasant or ugly. The purpose of each and every dream is self-discovery and awareness. You can use your dreams as tools to understand where you fit into this world and how to navigate your way through life. Your dreams tell you what you want to know the most… who you are and what you are really thinking, feeling or desiring. There is no good or bad, right or wrong. These are just your dreams delivering messages to you and giving you the opportunity to course correct as needed.

Conversely, if you are uncomfortable with what your dreams are revealing, and you feel you may act on them in a way that may be harmful to yourself or others, seek professional help immediately.

The next time you dream about a devil or demon, look at what this dream character is doing and notice how you feel about it. Identify the emotion and the action. Would you change anything if you could? Do you feel ashamed or proud? What has a hold on you, to where you feel you are not in control?

If I saw a devil in my dream, I would glean that it was a hidden desire or something trying to steer me off course. That would be my take. What is yours?

Devils in dreams can be very seductive, tempting and alluring. "Devil with a Blue Dress," "You're the Devil in Disguise." Do you recall the movie "Bedazzled" where Elizabeth Hurley is the sexy-as-all-get–out enchantress granting Brendan Fraser's character three wishes? A devil can represent temptation. Perhaps you are trying to be more health conscious with diet and exercise but the "devil" tempts you with fattening foods and points out that the couch looks inviting. Maybe you like to shop or gamble and want to cut back, but that darned pesky devil makes it hard for you to stick with your plan. What does this mean to you? Do you have a "devil may care" lackadaisical attitude and need to be a bit more disciplined and focused in your waking life? Are you not taking responsibility somewhere and passing the buck to someone else as in the case of "the devil made me do it"? A great example of the devil in a movie was Al Pacino's character in "The Devil's Advocate." Keanu Reeve's character was an up-and-coming young lawyer and his vice was vanity. The devil preyed on that and he gave in, which caused him considerable distress. Fortunately for him, it was all a dream and he had the chance to choose differently upon waking.

Do you feel you are being tempted, swayed or drawn into something that you know is not good for you? To dream of a devil or demon may be suggesting just that. Take a moment to reflect on the message from this character and what you can glean from it.

Here are two dreams from my readers and my take on them:

Dear Laura,

I am studying the Pagan and Wiccan paths. Both appeal to me on many levels. I also read the tarot. In my dream, I was doing a tarot card reading for a guy who seemed fairly normal at first. I only use one deck, the Rider Waite. In this reading, all kinds of really strange cards that I had not seen before kept coming from the deck. Finally, it just got so bizarre that I stopped and asked him what his religion was. He said that he was a Satanist, that he worships the devil!!! I did my best to just keep reading and try not to let it bother me, but it totally did bother me. After I was finished, he said that I was a good reader and that he would come back again and tell all his friends about me. In any other case, I would be stoked to hear that, but in this case, I was a little scared. The cards that kept coming from the deck were things like severed heads, beasts, blood… very grotesque and twisted. I just said "OK," and then I got the hell out of dodge! This guy was too

scary for me. I still do not know much about Satanists, what they do or how they do it or why, but the feeling I got was not good at all.

-Scared Stiff

Dear Scared Stiff,

I have done energy work and readings for people, so I can certainly relate to the dilemma that you faced in your dream of trying to be a compassionate professional and come from a place of non-judgment while preserving your energy and maintaining boundaries. You were clearly not comfortable with this client, as you were not in sync, and it would be a good idea to refer elsewhere had this been an actual client. However, given that this was not an actual client but a dream scenario, let's take a look at what this could mean for you. You are into Pagan and Wiccan beliefs, and he was a Satanist. I do not know a great deal about either, but from my understanding the Pagan and Wiccan religions are more about connecting with the earth and respecting mother nature, where Satanism is in direct opposition to Christianity. With that said, something about this man and his beliefs was making you feel ill at ease as evidenced by the tarot cards that came up... severed heads, beasts and blood. I would take this to mean that you may feel like you were giving your power away to the other person by drawing the card with blood. Blood is something that sustains our bodies, and this could mean that you felt your chi or "life force" was being drained by this energetic vampire. A severed head could mean that you were feeling disconnected energetically and wanted to be able to "keep your head on straight" with this client and retain your intense focus, where your strong emotions and need for self-preservation were distracting to you. Beasts can represent the shadow self or disowned parts of the psyche. So what was it about this man that threw you off kilter? Who or what does he represent? The cards are you looking without rather than within. Cards are known as tool of divination, however, from a dreaming perspective can be "house of cards" or "not in the cards" or "play your cards right." This dream may be a sign to check yourself and make sure that all is balanced and well within you before working closely with others, and to make sure to clear and separate their energy from yours and disconnect when the reading is complete. This was a powerful dream message, and I hope you will heed the advice from your higher self. As much as this client was distasteful to you, he sure seemed to be appreciative of your time and talent, so I would take this as a sign that you are on the right track, even if this is not your ideal type of client. The fact that he wanted to refer business to you is the ultimate compliment, however, unfortunately this is an energy you do not want to engage. You handed yourself well in the dream, which shows that you will do the same in real life. I would suggest doing a house clearing and have a chakra clearing session so that you can attract only the type of client you desire.

Dear Laura,

I dreamed that I was in a field of beautiful green grass dressed all in white; it was a serene and beautiful scene. I saw a bunch of people who looked really scared, also dressed in white. They ran toward me and said "Vicki, we are so happy you are here, the demons are trying to take us to to hell." I knew they were innocent souls, so I told them to stand behind me and I began chanting "LEAVE ALL THE CHILDREN ALONE LEST YOU BE TURNED TO STONE." I kept chanting and I saw the beast... he was bloody with big claws and yellow eyes, pointy ears and he was growling, snorting and his breath smelled like death.

I could hear him thinking he was going to take us to hell, and I just kept chanting. He snorted and ran off, and I ran after him. He turned to stone and broke into pieces. Then I woke up. I wonder what that was all about, and I still remember the chant.

-Pretty Vicki

Dear Pretty Vicki,

This vividly detailed dream has many dimensions to it. The white may symbolize purity, and the green health or healing. The fact you are in the grass suggests a desire to be closer to nature. The people in white are also aspects of yourself. I love how you easily fend off the demon and watch him shatter into tiny pieces. That shows me that you will handle any negative situation that arises with ease.

Who is currently trying to "make your life a living hell" or giving you grief? I get the sense that maybe something or someone from your past is trying to resurface and tempt you back into doing something you don't want to do or be. You have the knowledge and the resources to overcome, as evidenced by the chant you so easily recounted. You have strong leadership skills, and I love how you asked the people to stand behind you, stepping up and taking charge. What is it that you are wanting to put behind you, Vicki? A vacation to someplace where you can have some peace and quiet may be in order.

Chapter Four: Monsters, Goblins, Scary Clowns and More

In the previous chapter, we discussed devils and demons in dreams. In this chapter, we will talk about the appearance of monsters, goblins, scary clowns and other freaky or weird dream characters. I have no particular aversion to dolls, puppets or clowns, however, a lot of people find them truly scary. In the movie "Saw" there is a character called the "Jigsaw" who looks like a spooky clown, and let's not forget the movie "Child's Play" with creepy "Chucky" doll that are utterly terrifying to some. There is also a movie called "Pumpkin Head," which is self explanatory, and I am certain there were some episodes of "Night Gallery" that featured voodoo dolls that come to life and go on killing sprees. There was a show called the "Twilight Zone" that was very popular in the '70s and '80s and there were pig-faced people, talking dolls, possessed typewriters, as well as evil children who could read your thoughts and kill you with the blink of an eye. And last but certainly not least... I have to mention Stephen King, with "Pet Semetary," which featured dead animals that came back to life similar to the walking dead and the movie "Christine" about the sports car that was in love with its owner and killed to please him. And, of course, the most popular of them all for many years was vampires and even more recently, zombies! You have probably seen every variety of this theme: zombie strippers, zombie hookers, zombie dog walkers, zombie nannies, the list goes on.

What do all of these very different dream characters have in common? The answer is you, the dreamer. Most of these characters are manufactured images from Hollywood that have been deeply embedded in your subconscious mind, paired with emotions from childhood memories. Let's say, for example, that your older brother used to lock you in the closet and there were porcelain dolls with white faces inside of the closet that looked very scary in the dark. Years later, you see a movie as an adult that features dolls similar to what you saw as a child, or perhaps you are in a store and see a doll that looks just like the one you saw in the closet. Guess what you will be dreaming about tonight? If you guessed the scary doll, you are correct! You will probably have a nightmare about it, as there are some powerful emotions attached to that image, and seeing it triggered that memory for you. Never fear! This is not something that exists outside of you and your experiences… so it cannot hurt you, as we discussed in Chapter Three. These are your dreams and your fears, coming from your own memories. It really is as simple as that!

So what does it mean to see one or more of these characters show up in your dream? A clown can mean something different to someone who is deathly afraid of them versus someone who collects them. Maybe it is a fear that you need to overcome, or perhaps the clown is representing a co-worker who is not doing their fair share or "clowning around" and is distracting to you, for example. The clown could be a messenger sent to tell you that you need to "lighten up a bit" and play more. If it is a sad clown, he may be telling you that it is OK to express yourself and you do not have to put on a false front for others, or maybe even alerting you to someone in your life who acts as the sad clown does, smiling on the outside, miserable on the inside. Dream images can have as many meanings as there are dreamers; it is entirely subject to the interpretation of the individual.

At the risk of sounding flip, lazy or unoriginal, I always say that you, the dreamer, are your own best authority on your dreams. With that said, let's take a moment to reflect on the interesting array of characters in this chapter. Clowns, goblins, monsters, dolls, puppets, vampires, zombies, etc. Are there any from the list that stand out to you just now? If so, which ones and what about them attracts or repels you? Vampires have been very romanticized by movies like the "Twilight" saga, "Interview with the Vampire" and HBO's popular "True Blood" series. I am thinking vampires are probably more fantasized about and revered than truly feared in recent times, due to them being made so appealing by the film industry.

The following is a dream about puppets from one of my readers and my take on it.

Dear Laura,

When I was small, I used to watch "Sesame Street" every day. I loved that show up until I started having nightmares about Bert and Ernie. I would dream that Bert, the bald one, was whispering to Ernie and they were conspiring to make me bald like Bert! It got so bad that I would run and hide behind the sofa whenever Bert and Ernie came on and was even afraid to get my hair cut. I thought if I stepped foot in a barber shop I would end up fully bald just like Bert! My mom tried to tell me they were only puppets and it was all just a bad dream, but it took me a long, long time to get over being afraid of Bert and Ernie, barber shops and bald people.

-Beware of the Bald Man

Dear Beware,

Wow. That does sound traumatic for a small child to have such a vivid dream, and I can surely feel empathy for how scared you were and for so long! It sounds as if this dream actually created a phobia around hair loss and bald people. I am guessing you were about 5 or 6 when this dream occurred, and while I do not know what your home life was like at this time, I would venture to say that there was a certain bald man who was not to your liking. Somehow, you got the notion that being bald was a bad thing and to be avoided! Perhaps you heard them discussing how men lose hair as they as age and voicing their negative opinions about baldness in general. There may have been other characters from TV or movies that were "bad guys" or "villains" who were also bald. I do recall the story from the Bible that was made into a movie about Sampson, the strong man, who lost his strength when his hair was cut off by Delilah. Perhaps you heard the story or saw the movie and somehow these dots all connected in your subconscious, manifesting in a nightmare about baldness. At any rate, this dream affected you profoundly, yet you did manage to overcome your fear. I wish I had know you then, as I would have guided you to speak to Bert, find out who he represented and get him to tell you why he wanted you to be bald. I would also ask you what was so bad about baldness and what specifically bothered you about it. Well, I am glad to hear that you were able to move past this fear.

Dear Laura,

I used to have a recurring dream when I was a little tyke, no more than 3 or 4. The dream mysteriously stopped around the age of 6. In the dream, there was a duck with a pot stuck on his head, running around quacking while trying desperately to get it off. At the time, I found this dream to be very disturbing, and I still remember it so vividly. I would like your expert opinion, please.

-Duckman

Dear Duckman,

It is amazing how well we can recall certain dreams regardless of how much time has passed, while others elude us completely. This dream image does seem rather humorous, however, to a young child it must have been terrifying. If you go back and revisit that time of your life, I am sure that you will be able to remember some of the events from that period. Perhaps there was extreme tension and discord within the family unit? I am sensing that the duck was you and being that you were so young at the time when you first had this dream, you were not able to express your fears, frustrations or concerns. A duck is an animal that appears calm above the surface, while the feet are moving very fast below the surface. Does the term "sitting duck" apply here? I think it does, and it shows you were powerless to do anything about what was happening around you. The pot over the head suggests that you felt you were not able to see, hear or speak about what was going on in the home. Perhaps talking to a trusted and willing family member or doing some regression therapy will help to lend more clarity.

If you see any of these aforementioned characters in your dream, look at the character and observe the action. What are they doing? What are you doing? What is the feeling in the dream, is it tense or relaxed? Do you feel the same upon waking? How do you feel about this character, a goblin for example? Do you find them cute or scary? Monsters can be frightening, but to dream of Frankenstein would probably not be, as he was a popular movie and TV character. He would probably be more of an ally than a threat if he appeared in a dream, depending on your thoughts about him. There is a reason that they have chosen to show up in your dream and, while I am here to guide you, it is ultimately up to you to crack the code and decipher the message, as only you can speak your unique dream language. Look at the dream character more closely and determine who or what they represent and what they want you to know.

Chapter Five: Menacing or Opposing Figures in Dreams (Snakes, Spiders, Mobsters, Killers)

In the previous chapter, we discussed monsters, goblins and clowns in dreams. In this chapter, we will determine which characters you find most scary or undesirable when they appear in your dreams. I have found vicious dogs, angry mobs and, at times, movie characters to be opposing figures when they star in my dreams. They can be characters that you know (abusive parent or teacher for example) or they can be characters that are portrayed as scary from books or movies.

I recall a character from Harper Lee's classic book "To Kill a Mockingbird" known as Boo Radley. He was a man who was mentally unstable and basically a shut in. The neighborhood kids had never seen him, of course, so they let their imaginations run wild, convincing themselves that he was a psychotic killer and someone to be avoided at all costs. It turned out he was nothing like they feared, however, the mind is so powerful it can convince us of anything if we let our imaginations run far enough. This is also true of our dreaming mind. We may encounter a gruff stranger at the gas station and then somehow he appears in our dream as a machete wielding maniac. This is our own doing, seeing something we view as a negative and imposing it onto a real-life person. This is a manifestation of our fears.

It does not matter who the menacing figure or what the opposition is, because they are always here to teach us something important. There is not much difference between Mike Myers from the "Halloween" series or a pit of snakes or spiders. While they may be scary and not fun to see in a dream, the upside is that you get to wake up and they will be gone. I hope that before you do wake up, that you will get the message they have prepared just for you. They would not be in your dream if they did not have something for you. How can a South American drug lord like Pablo Escobar be beneficial to you? If he appears in your dream, I guarantee you that he absolutely can be to your benefit.

It is important that you take note of what is happening in the dream. What are you doing and what are they are doing? Are they chasing and you running, for example? Are you engaged in a battle of some sort? What words do they use, if any? Do you find people or animals more of a threat when they appear in your dream? For me, it would be animals, as I feel like people would be easier to escape or kill, if necessary. I could take a man down more easily than I could a saber-toothed tiger or bear.

In addition to asking yourself who this person or animal is and what is happening in the dream, next ask yourself how you feel about them specifically. Some people are extremely fearful of snakes or spiders to the point of being phobic. Some would just find them inconvenient, while some will even have them as pets. These are three different perceptions that people may have about the same thing. If it is a person, say a serial killer or rapist... is this someone who is on the loose and in your area, or is this someone who is safely behind bars and not eligible for parole like Charles Manson? It is important to examine your relationship to this dream character. If it is indeed Charles Manson, then unless your family was one of his victims or followers, you probably do not have a connection to him.

My relationship to him is that he is not someone I would ever be within 100 feet of.

Here are a few dreams from readers:

Dear Laura,

I had a dream that my boyfriend and I were walking around Pender Island. All of a sudden, a vicious gang attacked us. They had guns and bombs. We managed to get away in a cab, yet people were being hurt and killed everywhere. What could this mean?

-Lydia

Dear Lydia,

This dream suggests an imbalance of male and female energy and the feeling that you are not in control of some area in your life. Perhaps you fear losing your identity or power in this relationship? Also, there may be interference from friends and family, or a sense of being "ganged up" on. The fact that you got away shows that you do feel confident in your ability to handle any such situation. Getting into a cab implies that you trust someone you do not know well to get you to safety. Guns can be phallic symbols, definitely male. To be held at gunpoint would denote that you may be feeling cornered or like your hand is being forced. How does this apply? When a bomb goes off, it creates chaos and destruction, so maybe you feel like you have to drop a bomb on someone (an unwanted pregnancy, for example), someone dropped a bomb on you recently or maybe you are simply feeling like you are about to explode? Seeing the other people being hurt and killed may suggest that you are feeling vulnerable in some way, yet in this dream you were able to get away unscathed, which is a very good sign that you will overcome obstacles in your daily life. The general tone of this dream is one of others dictating to you or calling the shots, and you are feeling powerless. This is something to think about because this is causing inner turmoil to you, as depicted in your dream.

Dear Laura,

I have a lot of dreams, now more than ever, about being bitten by snakes, and I can actually feel the bites in my dreams. I also have lots of dreams where someone close to me is always putting spiders on me or trying to. These are not good dreams! Can you help me to understand why I would be dreaming this?

-Arachnophobia

Dear Arachnophobia,

Judging by the tone of your letter, I am guessing that snakes and spiders are not your favorite members of the animal kingdom! It appears that in your case, a snake bite could be some "snaky" behavior reflecting back on you. Have you been a gossip or stabbed even one person in the back? Perhaps you feel others are doing this to you? This dream could also be a warning that someone in your circle is not acting in your best interest, and further involvement with this person could lead to considerable heartache. Loved ones putting spiders on you has much the same effect as the snake bite; someone close to you doing something to you that you do not want them to do. This suggests a sense of your boundaries being violated, and this could be in the form of blame, judgment, ridicule, criticism or anything that you deem unpleasant or unwanted. It may be a good idea to keep your friends close and your enemies closer for a while, and really watch and observe what they do, as actions speak louder than words. Our dreams oftentimes serve as forewarnings of what is to come.

Dear Laura,

My wife keeps having a dream where she vomits live snakes or fish, but never both at the same time. She is disgusted by this, of course, yet no one else seems to think too much of it. Weird, huh?

-Jake

Dear Jake,

No, this is not weird at all, as to vomit is to purge oneself. Your wife may be wanting to rid herself of some negative energy or habits that are not serving her. In the Bible, fish represent spiritual nourishment and snakes are the serpentine energy, which is considered evil. Perhaps she is feeling that something bad always has to follow something good? I noticed that she is vomiting live snakes and fish rather than dead ones. That is significant. These animals are still retaining their life force after being in her stomach for a period of time, and this denotes survival despite the odds. This may be a sign that she will overcome some serious obstacles or challenges or may be in the process of doing so. There may be some health issues that she is unaware of, so a visit to a health professional is always a good idea, as sometimes our dreams alert us to potential problems or early stages of illness. The fact that she is upset, yet no one else seems phased, can mean that she is being overly sensitive or perhaps the people in her life are not being sensitive enough. To you and to your wife this dream seem weird, however, this is telling your wife something about herself that she needs to know. Where do you feel you fit into this equation? Do you need to be more sensitive to her needs or do you feel she tends to overreact and blow things out of proportion? Is someone being snaky or fishing for something? Dreams can be quite literal at times.

Chapter Six: Just Plain Scary Dreams (Situations That You Fear)

In the previous chapter, we discussed scary people and what roles they play in our lives. In this chapter, I want to address stressful situations rather than specific people. We will look at which dreams really freak you out or annoy you and why you keep having them. Do you dread going to sleep because of a particular recurrent dream? Is there one that causes you to wake up in a panic? Is it being broke? Death or dying? Your partner being unfaithful? Your child being bullied or using drugs? Being late for work or school? Naked in public? Teeth falling out? Car accident? Natural disaster?

The nature of your dream is less important than *how you feel about it upon waking.* Waking up feeling disappointed that your husband is not Channing Tatum but the lump snoring next to you or that you did not win the lottery is not cause for concern, in my opinion. Those are wishful-thinking dreams and fun to have. What would make me think something was amiss is a strong reaction like anger, sadness, intense fear or extreme relief that it was "just a dream." The way you are feeling during the dream versus after the dream is very telling. Are you sad the dream is over or are you thankful?

What you fear, whether conscious or not, will play out in your dreams. It is very common to have recurrent dreams of this nature. When this happens, it is your subconscious mind or higher self telling you about you. It means there is something that you are repressing or struggling with and there is more work to be done with this particular theme or issue. Go ahead and ignore it all you want. It will just come back stronger and with more frequency until you are ready to listen to the message your dream is so desperately trying to send to you. It is nothing to be scared of, as it is coming from you and no one else. Your subconscious mind and higher self are a part of you and the better, more evolved parts, in my opinion. The ego or personality operates from fear while the higher self knows better.

So what is keeping you awake at night? What is the worst-case scenario you are dreaming of? No matter what it is, nothing is too scary to admit to. Nothing. It may seem horrific to admit to yourself that you had a dream that you left your dog in the hot car and it died. This does not make you a bad person or irresponsible pet owner. It means that you may be overlooking something important, and your dream is trying to give you a much-needed wake up call. It may be telling you to slow down and pay attention to what is going in your daily life, as you are clearly missing some important details. If you have a dog, the interpretation may be more literal than if you have no pets. If you do not have a dog, then it may mean something else, such as you are not sure you are ready for the responsibility of caring for someone or being in charge, that you are afraid you will mess it up. It could also mean that you are trying to kill off a part of yourself that you dislike. Men are sometimes referred to as dogs, if they are the Casanova types. Certain not-so-nice behaviors can be described as "dogging someone." These are just a few possible meanings for this dream, and there are many others.

What if you dream that you killed someone, a friend or family member, for example? Does that mean that you are about to embark on a killing spree? Unless you are a homicidal maniac, then your dream may just be a way to release frustration or disown parts of the self.

Let's look at some other dream themes that might be unpleasant. I have been out of school for many years, however, still to this day I will have the dream that I am late for class on my first day and can't find the building or that the semester is almost over and there was a very important paper, assignment or test that I forgot about or somehow missed, and I am scrambling to get it taken care of, so that I can complete the course with a passing grade. I call this an "anxiety dream." When I have this dream, I know that I am feeling challenged or unprepared in some way. I can usually pinpoint the source of my anxiety and address it when I wake up. I hate this dream, by the way! As much as I know dreams are precious gifts, this one always leaves me feeling rattled.

What is great about these scary dreams is that you do wake up from them.

To dream of falling is a very common fear-based dream. To have this dream usually means that you are not feeling in control of yourself or your circumstances. You do not feel like your feet are on solid ground or perhaps you are engaging in some behavior that could have negative consequences and cause you to "take a fall," either personally or professionally. If you dream you are in a car crash, it may be a sign that you are heading in the wrong direction or need to slow down. It is always good to check in and take inventory by asking yourself how this dream correlates to what you are dealing with or doing on a daily basis. It could be something so simple as a reminder to get your vehicle serviced. If your mind dreamed it and you remembered it, the answer is right there in front of you. It may take a minute to decode it, however, if it invokes a strong or unpleasant reaction, then chances are you know the hidden meaning in your dream. A good question to ask yourself when you have a dream that is less than desirable is "What would this mean to me and my loved ones if this were to come true?"

If you do not like what you are dreaming about and you are relieved when you wake up that is was just a dream, this is telling you something is out of alignment and giving you the choice to bring this into your current reality or not. For example, if you dream that you are having an affair and you get caught and your life falls apart, then it should be obvious what you need to do or stop doing. Oftentimes, the dream will not be so literal; it will come across as a little more cryptic. You may dream that your teeth are falling out or that you got a really bad haircut or something that you would not want to happen that would make you "lose face" or look bad somehow. This is a more subtle sign that you need to be careful about what you are creating, if this is not the desired result, or how you want to present yourself to the world. A more literal interpretation could be that you need to see a dentist, or perhaps the stylist you are thinking of going to is not a good fit for you.

I used to feel very anxious whenever I had the dream that I was married with a bunch of kids when I was in my late teens. At the time, it meant that I feared being trapped or stuck. I did eventually get married when I was older, however, at the time I was having the unpleasant dream about marriage and kids was when my parents were divorcing and there was a lot of turmoil in the home. My two younger brothers were still living at home and I was attending college when I first started having this dream. My mother had a lot on her plate, adjusting to all of the changes in such a short time, and I recall it was not a pleasant experience for any of us. It was a very stressful period in all of our lives. My dream was clearly mirroring my desire to avoid being in that situation at all costs, hence the flight or fight reaction my body would experience each time I had this dream. It was a useful dream, as I chose a man who was the polar opposite of my father when I got married.

The gift of scary dreams is that you do not have to live in them or accept this as your reality. You can wake up and choose differently.

Chapter Seven: Facing Your Fears With Lucid Dreaming

What do you fear most? What keeps you awake at night or causes you to have bad dreams? What is your waking nightmare? Is it being jobless, homeless, getting a divorce, losing a child, dying of cancer? Some fears you are probably acutely aware of, while others may be things you have repressed from your past. For example, if you were abused or molested as a child, you probably do not think of that daily, yet the dreaming mind has a way of bringing these fears to the forefront. You can confront your abuser in the dream and stop dreaming of them once and for all, as you have now faced your fear. Does this sound impossible to you? I am going to show you that it is more than possible, and dreams are something you can use to your advantage, and not something you are plagued by or a victim of. Your dreams can serve as guides and tools to assist you on your journey.

In the previous chapter, we discussed some scary dream themes, why we have them and what to do with them. In this chapter, I would like to go a step further and show you how to battle your inner demons simply by dreaming of them. Yes! You can conjure a certain or specific dream or dream character willingly, and you can be aware and involved in the process. You can steer the car, slay the dragon or grab the pot of gold in your dream and be aware that you have this power the whole time you are dreaming! How do you do this? It is called lucid dreaming. While you may not have any recollection of ever having done so, you have had lucid dreams before, as we all have.

Some would call it a dream within a dream, and some are aware that they are dreaming and are semi-awake.

A good example of a lucid dream would be if you were to fall off a cliff and suddenly sprouted wings and were able to fly. Another example of lucid dreaming might be if you felt your car going over the edge and you grabbed the steering wheel and swerved to safety just in the nick of time. This is not the same thing as when you fall asleep on the couch after the movie ends, and your body jerks and twitches causing you to wake up. That is just a physiological response to being uncomfortable and hearing static in the background. Lucid dreaming is much more than that! It is remaining in the dream state and being able to call people in or cast them out as you see fit, to be able to summon whatever skills or resources you need at the moment, without hesitation and everything is at your command!

You can dissolve your deepest, darkest fears through lucid dreaming. You can have those difficult conversations or confront those unpleasant feelings by using this method. It is truly amazing that when one is engaged in the act of lucid dreaming that nothing is out of reach, and there is always a solution to any situation or problem that arises. You will always have complete and total confidence and know exactly what to do and how to do it when you are having a lucid dream experience. Hesitation and doubt are products of the conscious or critical mind, and they are simply not present with lucid dreaming.

If there is a specific fear that you have, invite it to join you in the dream world. Let's say, for example, that you fear being broke and homeless. What do you see when this happens in the dream state? Is there a person there other than yourself or it is just an energy or feeling? Does this fear have a name? If not, give it a name. You can talk to it directly and ask it what it wants from you. Is there something you need to do? Someone you need to forgive? If you are not intent on a specific dream and one should happen spontaneously, stop and remember that you have the power to guide the dream in any direction that you wish. You are aware of how lucid dreaming works because you are reading about it now and have experienced it before. Set your intention so when you are having this experience, you will automatically recognize that you are in a lucid dream and slay the dragon, steer the car or fly away. You will remember that you can do anything you want or draw any person, dead or alive into your lucid dream. There are absolutely no limits to what the mind can accomplish for a lucid dreamer!

A wonderful lucid dream that I had several years ago has stayed with me. I still feel empowered by it each time that I recall it. This happened around the time that I was working as a freelance artist and recently divorced. I suppose I was feeling a little unsure of how I would get by at that time. I was used to being married and having two incomes and was now alone and with only myself to rely on. In the dream, I was in an alley and being cornered by an angry mob. The mob was closing in on me, and I knew I was in serious danger. My back was to the wall, and I had nowhere to hide and nothing to defend myself with, no weapon of any sort. I knew that if I showed any fear, cowered or tried to run I was dead meat. At that very moment, the only thing left for me to do was to get into a fighting stance and let out a very deep and loud yell. I harnessed my chi and went for it! The crowd immediately lost interest in me and dissipated. At that moment, I knew I was prepared to handle anything that came my way, no matter what. That was a very powerful and life-changing dream. I remember it often when I am feeling unsure about something. It serves as a reminder that I can handle anything and everything, as my higher self will give me the necessary tools at precisely the right time.

Sometimes we will draw the right people into our dreams to serve as guides or helpers. I was struggling with some self-image and boundary issues, and Jack Nicholson appeared in my dream. He had stopped by unannounced, and I was flustered and apologetic for not being more prepared for company. He grabbed my arm and said sternly, "Do not ever apologize for being who you are and especially not in your own damn house!" That stuck with me as well, and was the vote of confidence and affirmation I needed at the time. I consider that another form of a lucid dream. I drew him in, someone I consider strong, to deliver a powerful message. I was very sensory aware (another sign of lucid dreaming), as I could actually feel his hand grabbing my arm and, after he spoke to me, I just relaxed and went about my business as usual. This was a very empowering dream and an example of how you can use your dreams to face your fears, directly or indirectly, and feel more confident in your waking life.

Chapter Eight: Dream Journal Exercises

You may have noticed that chapter one was a repeat from book one. I did that purposely, just to reiterate the importance of dreams and why we have them, and in case the books were read separately or out of sequence. Sometimes information bears repeating and, in this case, I believe it does. With this chapter, I will not repeat all of the dream journal exercises from book one or book three because this book is very different from the others. Therefore, the exercises will be different as well. Before you groan and say this sounds like a lot of work, it really is not. In as little as 15 minutes a day, you can be well on your way to being an expert interpreter of your dreams and perhaps be of assistance to others. If you think of dream interpretation like a muscle, it becomes stronger the more that you work it. If you are reading this book or series, you are wanting to get more meaning from your dreams. It is really very simple and easy to do if you just make it a habit to record your dreams and define them. Here are some steps to help you get started.

1. Designate a dream journal: It is very important to have a sacred place to store your very unique gifts, otherwise known as dreams. It does not have to be fancy or expensive, but if it is appealing to look at, you will be more inclined to want to write in it. You can create one yourself, purchase one or use my free online journal at www.inyourdreamsbooks.com. You may want to use a special pen and perhaps have an

aromatherapy candle to go with it, to make recording your dreams an enticing ritual.

2. Get acquainted with your dream characters: Monster, goblins, devils, demons, spiders, snakes… these are not your neighbors, co-workers, grocer or people that you come in contact with daily, however, they may represent aspects of them. Determine who or what each character represents so that when you see them in subsequent dreams, you will recognize and remember them with ease. If the snake truly is your co-worker, for example, you will know to be extra careful around her and watch for information about her while dreaming and awake, as there will be more to come!

3. Face your fears: Ask yourself what is the worst-case scenario and, if it were to become your reality, how would you handle it? If you woke up and found your home infested with snakes or spiders, you would take immediate action and call a professional! How would the action you took in your dream be different from what you would do in your waking life? These are good questions to ask your dreaming versus waking self. If you found out your spouse was being unfaithful would the dream reaction and waking reaction be the same? Is there something you are being warned about in your dreams that you can take steps to safeguard yourself or your home to prevent from happening? For example, do you

need to child proof your home or install an alarm? Let your dreams be your guide.

4. Ask quality questions: As you sit before your journal ask, "What is the message for me in this dream?" If the answers come easily, by all means, jot them down. If your page is still blank after several minutes, try asking different questions. What do I need to know? What am I supposed to learn or to do differently? If nothing is coming to you after five minutes or so, then program yourself to have this dream message be made clear to you in a subsequent dream.

5. Set your intention before dreaming: "Tonight, I will dream of the scary clown and find out why he is chasing me" is a good example. When you see that character in your dream again, which you will if you summon it, do not let him get away without sharing his message! Stop and face the clown rather than running away as you have before. What does he have to tell you? Listen and take note. He will talk to you because he is a part of you. Pay attention!

6. Give thanks to your dreams and dream characters: I know you may be thinking it is crazy to have gratitude for a knife-wielding maniac, however, I assure you that if there is a message to be received, it is something that is of benefit to you. Now that you know that the message and gift are, be sure to take a moment to express gratitude to your

higher self for showing you something important. You can say it in your mind or out loud, or write it down… just be sure that you offer thanks and praise so that more dreams will be forthcoming.

Conclusion

I hope that you have enjoyed reading the second book in my three-part series about dreams as much as I have enjoyed writing them. If you have not read part one, "Your Dreams of Sex, Love and Romance and What They Mean," I hope that you will. In summary, I sincerely hope that you learned that nothing that you dream is truly scary. Nightmares have no power once you understand the meaning behind them. I hope that you will learn to use your bad or unpleasant dreams as tools to gain greater awareness into yourself and to make better choices in life. If you have interest in learning more about dark spirits and clearing them from your home, look for my book coming out in 2016 called "Living Harmoniously With the Spirit World" on Amazon and Lulu. Please like and share my page on Facebook, "In Your Dreams by Laura Suzanne." I also have a blog called "In Your Dreams," at www.inyourdreamsbooks.wordpress.com, and a website, www.inyourdreamsbooks.com. Stay tuned for book three, about dreams of money, luck and success, which will be out by December 2015.

Author Bio

Laura Suzanne Snell was born and raised in the San Francisco Bay Area and now resides in Las Vegas, with her beloved cat, Tiger. Laura is a graduate of San Diego State University where she received a Bachelor of Science degree in Psychology. A lifelong student of parapsychology and metaphysical enthusiast, Laura has read many books on the subject of dreams and further expanded her knowledge by taking additional courses through the Dream Interpretation Institute and by becoming a Certified Dream Guide. Curious to learn even more about the inner workings of the subconscious mind, Ms. Snell enrolled in courses at Serenus Clinical Hypnosis and added Certified Clinical Hypnotherapist to her resume. After having a profound experience with energetic healing that instantly cured her of a long-standing medical condition, she became a Certified Usui Reiki Master Practitioner/Teacher initiated by Susan Fox of Virginia.

Laura has written articles for Las Vegas Image Magazine and had a column featuring dream interpretation called "In Your Dreams" in Las Vegas Weekly. She has been a frequent guest on local radio stations, including KLAV and 97.1 The Point, in addition to co-hosting a radio show with Master Hypnotherapist Victoria Gallagher called"Hyptalk," where holistic health and metaphysics were the focus. She has taught classes and hosted workshops at bookstores and health food stores, such as Borders and Whole Foods in Las Vegas.

Laura is highly intuitive and empathic, making her a natural for assisting others in discovering the deeper meanings of even the most bizarre or complex dreams. Let her be your guide to solving the mystery of your dreams by reading her book series and following the do it yourself instructions, tips and suggestions she has provided for you. You will find that with a little effort you will soon become a pro at decoding your own dreams and that is her wish for you.

www.ingramcontent.com/pod-product-compliance
Lightning Source LLC
Chambersburg PA
CBHW022343040426
42449CB00006B/693